5 EASY WAYS TO INCREASE YOUR PROFITS TODAY

A Simple "Secret" Formula to Massively Grow Profits In Any Business

By Chris Gold

Is there a "secret" way to grow your profits?

Many business coaches have taught a simple, "secret" formula to massively grow profits in any business to business owners.

Interestingly, those owners in the category of small-and-medium sized businesses seem to embrace this formula far easier than those "big business" owners who have been in business for a long time.

Since good business knowledge is one of the key elements to business success, the more knowledge I would like to help you "re-educate" yourself and your team on how to run a more profitable business, the more comfortable you will become with the idea of coaching, and the more open you may be to some of the other systems and strategies available.

There is "Magic" in Numbers

Be aware of one thing, however.

The following "formula" is based on a series of profit "drivers" — best explained by simple numbers and formulas.

If you are "number phobic," don't worry.

The examples are simple and easy to follow.

However, know that as an owner, there is "magic" in knowing numbers — from what your numbers in your business really are — to how new sets of numbers can literally add thousands, or even hundreds of thousands of dollars to your bottom-line.

When you can become a master of your numbers (because, after all, the language of business is numbers), you will see vast improvements in your business and in the opportunities presented to you.

And, when you are comfortable with the numbers in the "secret" formula, you will be ready and able to work all the factors in the equation.

Then, you'll start seeing more bottom-line growth and profit than you — and your competitors — could ever imagine.

CONTENTS

Title Page

CHAPTER 1 THE "5 WAYS"... WHAT IT IS AND HOW IT WORKS FOR YOUR BOTTOM-LINE.	1
CHAPTER 2 HOW TO APPLY THE "5 WAYS" TO YOUR COMPANY.	3
CHAPTER 3 THE 7 BIG QUESTIONS & ANSWERS OF BUSINESS SUCCESS.	6
CHAPTER 4 THE FIRST QUESTION IS WHAT?	9
CHAPTER 5 THE SECOND BIG QUESTION IS WHO?	11
CHAPTER 6 BIG QUESTION 3 IS HOW?	13
CHAPTER 7 THE FOURTH BIG QUESTION OF BUSINESS SUCCESS IS WHERE?	15
CHAPTER 7 THE SIXTH BIG QUESTION OF BUSINESS SUCCESS IS WHY?	19
CHAPTER 8 THE SEVENTH BIG QUESTION OF BUSINESS SUCCESS IS HOW MANY?	21
CHAPTER 9 THERE ARE A FEW POINTS I WANT TO EMPHASIZE.	24
CHAPTER 10 MEET THE PERFECT CUSTOMER LIFECYCLE	27
STEP 1: Attract Traffic	28
STEP 2 Capture Leads	31
STEP 3: Nurture Prospects	33

STEP 4: Convert Sales	35
STEP 5: Deliver and Satisfy	37
STEP 6: Upsell Customers	39
STEP 7: Get Referrals	40

CHAPTER 1 THE "5 WAYS" ... WHAT IT IS AND HOW IT WORKS FOR YOUR BOTTOM-LINE.

So, what is this simple growth and profit-focused formula?

While most people see profits based only on two factors (revenues and costs), the "5 Ways" sees profit based on 5 separate profit drivers.

Just with a few simple distinctions, the "5 Ways" gives you 2.5 times more options to work on your profit — giving you 2.5 times more opportunity boost your profits - versus other "expert" owners who love to "cut their way" on the expense side to boost their profits.

What are those factors? Very simply:

Leads. This is the total number of leads — those people who have contacted or who have been contacted by the business — over the course of a year.

Conversion rate. This is the percentage of people who actually bought. For example, if 10 people walk through a store and three people buy something, that store's conversion rate of 3 out of 10, or 30%, for that day.

Average dollar sale. This is the average dollar amount per sale — estimated over the course of a year. It's just an average and can range from $5 or $10 (say for a discount retailer) up to tens of thousands of dollars (say for a car dealership).

Average number of transactions. This is the number of purchases the average customer will make over the course of a year. Again, this can be an estimate. In a retail setting, this will probably be larger than those companies that operate in a professional services industry.

Profit margin. This is the profit percentage of each and every sale. Simply put, if a business sells something for $100, and profit was $25, the profit margin is 25%.

So how does this all relate to top line revenue and bottom-line profit?

Let's see.

CHAPTER 2 HOW TO APPLY THE "5 WAYS" TO YOUR COMPANY.

In your sample company, we can use a very simple formula to multiply the factors we've just discussed.

Remember, this formula multiplies factors, not just adds them. That means the cumulative impact on the bottom-line is massive.

The "5 Ways" formula looks like this:

Leads x Conversion Rate = Customers

Customers x Avg. Value/Dollar Sale x Number of Transactions = Revenue

Revenue x Profit Margins = Profit

In your company, let's say you have either estimated or fully determined the following numbers:

4,000 x 25% = 1000 Customers 1000 x $100 x 2 = $200,000 Revenue $200,000 x 25%
= $50,000 Profit

What does all of this mean?

Simply put, you are running a business that converts 1 in 4 prospects into paying customers, and those customers average two purchases at $100 per purchase each year — and your company enjoys a 25% profit margin on revenues of $200,000.

It also means your total profit for the year is $50,000.

So, what would happen if, over the course of the next year, you could increase results by just 10% in each of the 5 areas?

Let's do it, and then let's take a look at what happens to your bottom line:

4,400 x 27.5% = 1210 Customers 1210 x $110 x 2.2 = $292,820 Revenue $292,820 x 27.5% = $80,525.50 Profit

How a 10% Increase in Top-Line Revenue Becomes a 61% Increase in Profit

Examine the numbers closely and you'll see the 10% increase is incremental -which means you could easily nudge numbers up by that amount over a period of months — or even weeks.

The bottom-line is that the new bottom-line looks very interesting, doesn't it?

Even though we've increased each factor by just 10% (including top line revenue), we were able to boost bottom-line profit by 61% — or a total of $30,525.50.

What could you do with an extra $30,000 in your business this year?

Think 10% is impressive?

Do some math on your own and see what the numbers look like if you increase 30%, 50% or even 100% down the line.

The key is that we are multiplying factors — not adding — which has a massive impact on profit.

Contrary to those "mature" and "expert" business owners, the "5 Ways" isn't a complicated numbers game.

It's simply looking at your business in a different way and working a set of numbers that exist in every company.

While your competitors will be in an endless cycle of trying to grow top line revenue and cutting expenses to generate more profit, you'll have at least 5 other factors with which to work.

And there are literally hundreds of strategies you can use to boost those numbers immediately and over time.

If you want to do some extra homework, you can work your own numbers and brainstorm ways you could increase leads, get more customers coming back, increase what and the amount they buy and raise your profit margins.

Unlike some of your old homework from your school days, however, there can be a literal and immediate payoff to your efforts — in the form of literal dollars in your pocket.

Plus, you'll be miles ahead of the majority of owners successfully operating businesses today.

Better yet, you'll be pleasantly surprised how "mastering the numbers" is easy to do — and you'll be more than happy with your ultimate results.

CHAPTER 3 THE 7 BIG QUESTIONS & ANSWERS OF BUSINESS SUCCESS.

Let's take you through a way to make your business stand out in a crowded marketplace by answering the 7 big questions of business success, so that you create unique value for your customers. These questions are what, who, how, where, when, why and how many.

They are designed to shift your business away from having to focus on the question that stops so many businesses earning a good profit - how much does it cost?

In a market where customers perceive little difference between the products and services available from competitors, the key buying criteria is who has got the lowest price.

Nothing else matters.

But in markets where companies offer distinctive products and services which are not available from anyone else, then the importance of prices recedes into the background. I know a lot of business owners feel that customers only buy on price and even pride themselves on taking the same approach when they are buying but it's usually not true. To prove it, I'd like you to look around in your office, home or car.

Are you wearing the cheapest clothes and shoes that you can find, or did you spend more than you had to? Is the office equipment you use, like your PC, the cheapest available or did you spend more because of special features and benefits? Is your car a £100 old banger which is only just roadworthy, or did you spend more for prestige, comfort, speed and what it says about you?

When you had lunch today, did you buy the cheapest thing on the menu or the lowest priced sandwich or did you treat yourself to something a little bit special? Sure you may love a bargain - who doesn't. But what you buy often isn't the cheapest. There's some element of value which has convinced you that it is a good idea to pay more than the minimum.

And your customers are the same when they perceive a difference in the product or service. As I explain in my report, the Profit Tipping Point, price is important to the customer. A new Rolls Royce costing £250,000, which is a very differentiated product, is even nicer if you can buy with a 20% discount. But price is even more important to the supplier than the customer. That's because price is the number one driver of profit.

Provided you have a profitable business, a 5% increase in selling price will increase your profits more than a 5% increase in sales volumes or a 5% reduction in costs if nothing else changes. To convince customers and get higher prices you must differentiate your products in a way that customers value.

This is important.

It's not being different that matters. It's being different in ways that matter to your target customers. You may already claim that your business is different and if so, I have a little game for you to play.

I teach my clients that there are two types of marketing:

Outreach marketing where you reach out to prospective custom-

ers who may be interested and
Search marketing where potential customers are searching for something to buy and your job is to be found and create sufficient interest to be contacted.

We live in the Internet age and it has shifted the balance from outreach marketing designed to interrupt customers to search marketing, when customers look when they want to buy.

Yesterday I was sent in the mail three copies of a catalogue from an office furniture supplier. It wasn't very well targeted because I'm a one-man band and there's no way they should have sent me three copies. In the old days I may have kept one to refer to. Now if I want some (as I did last year when I bought a new office chair), I look on the Internet.

But there's a problem.

Just like Yellow Pages in the past, the Internet gathers up all your competitors together and if you are not careful, it creates a sea of sameness.

That's where my Marketing Bingo game comes in.
List down what you think are your key differentiators that you stress in your marketing and sales presentations and then go to Google and look at your competitors' websites.

You'll be horrified at how often the things that you thought made you different are also claimed by your competitors. And if customers think that all the products are the same, what happens? They decide to buy on price. Let's delve deeper into the seven big questions of business success.

CHAPTER 4 THE FIRST QUESTION IS WHAT?

Now what can be interpreted in different ways?

What unique products or services do you sell that no one else does? Perhaps you have unique distribution rights, or you have something designed and made especially for you?

An even bigger potential differentiator is what does your product do for customers? If you can offer a unique benefit - and if no one can copy it - then you have a significant advantage for those customers who value it.

Most products and services have big generic benefits - a car gets you from A to B, clothes keep you warm, protect your modesty and make you look good, one Television shows the same programs as the others. But sometimes you can find secondary benefits that appeal to a particular group of customers.

Saga Cruises specializes in old people. The ships still go from port to port and you can eat and drink from dawn to midnight, but Saga specialize in looking after the old, the infirm and the disabled.

The benefits also come through in my third what question. What special experiences do you deliver?

In Saga's case, it means that people can still enjoy cruising when they can't cope with normal cruise ships.

Differentiation often comes through creating an emotional bond and we get alerted to differences through our five senses - sight, sound, taste, smell and touch.

What senses can you stimulate in a unique way?

The looks of a car are important to me but I'm finding it much more difficult to tell modern cars apart. There is a sea of sameness, but it does mean that the cars I like the look of, stand out even more.

The senses can also be used to turn away potential customers. Differentiation is about creating polarization - being right for some and wrong for others.

I don't go near some stores because of the music being played, if it can be called music. I know that they are not my kind of place.

What can also refer to special ingredients? Both Coca-Cola and KFC, two huge international brands, are differentiated through secret recipes.

What can also refer to what's been taken out of the product? I've just come back from the dentist and he told me that if I have to eat sweets, I should be eating the sugar free varieties.

There are two very important "what" questions you can ask which help you to innovate.

What are your customers' particular wants, problems and needs?

And... What frustrates customers of yours, your competitors and substitutes when they are buying, storing, using or disposing of the product?

The better you understand your customers and why they buy and don't buy, the more you can design a better product set the customers' buying criteria to create preference in your favor.

CHAPTER 5 THE SECOND BIG QUESTION IS WHO?

Again, this question can be interpreted in a number of different ways. The obvious one is who are your customers?

Two of my coaching mastermind partners focus on narrow niches. Ian Brodie concentrates on coaches and consultants and Heather Townsend works with people who want to be or are partners in firms of accountants and lawyers.

It's an easy way to differentiate yourself from the more general competitors.

It's attractive to customers who know you understand their business and it means that you can tailor everything you do to suit the special needs of a tightly defined group.
The second part of who is the one area where I guarantee you are unique ... That's you.

No one else has the same special combination of education, skills, knowledge, experience, personality, attitudes and beliefs.
We live in a time when celebrity status is highly valued.

Gary Vaynerchuk is a great example. He's been called the first wine guru of the YouTube era because of his enthusiastic and passionate wine tasting videos, and they've sent sales soaring.
Or if you don't want to be a celebrity, you can still use the "power of who" and the attraction of star appeal by having a celebrity

promote and endorse your product.

It may seem a flimsy reason to create buyer preference to have Cheryl Cole promote L'Oreal hair products, but it works and you'll see the same idea repeated in many markets.

Yes, top stars will be expensive and are probably beyond your budget but what about actors who have left popular soaps and haven't enjoyed regular work since or retired sports stars. Their faces and names are still very well known.

The who theme can also be used on who are your staff.

The best example I can think of is Hooters, the restaurant chain where the waitresses are scantily clad, attractive young women. Hooters won't suit everybody, but it is strongly differentiated. Finally, on the who question, you can create differentiation by who does the work between the supplier and the customer.

I hate flat pack furniture but it's fundamental to how IKEA differentiates itself by stripping costs out of the manufacture and distribution process so budget conscious customers can buy modern furniture at low prices and assemble it themselves at home.

CHAPTER 6 BIG QUESTION 3 IS HOW?

How you deliver the products, service, benefits and experience to customers can set you apart from your competitors.

You do need to be a little careful.

I get cross when I hear marketing experts tell you to forget features and concentrate on the benefits.

Don't get me wrong.

Customers buy because of the benefits they will get, and you must answer the classic "what's in it for me?" question.

But features give the benefits credibility and tangibility.

You buy a new PC because it will improve your productivity and help you to get more done in less time.

You have confidence in buying it because it has the latest microchip from Intel.
The how has to be visible to customers and important to them.
I bet you don't care what software your accountants use to prepare your statutory accounts and tax returns.

But you may well choose one consultant over another because of particular proprietary techniques they use. You believe in the method, the how they do it.
Sometimes the how is essential to your purchase decision.

You may be terrified about going to the dentist and want more specialist treatment than the normal painkilling injection. Instead you can find a dentist who will shoot you full of valium, so you don't even hear the dreadful sound of the drill. Or perhaps you don't believe in drugs and insist on hypnotherapy to disguise the pain.

Or the how can be a way to enhance the experience.

I like flambé desserts done at the table like cherry jubilee or crepe Suzette because they are exciting and have a wow factor and I'll choose them if they appear on the menu.

How can also apply to a fundamental question like "how can you take away the buyer's risk?"

Many buyers have learnt to be cynical about marketing claims. The bigger the claim, the more they fear it's an exaggeration so how you give them a chance to experience the benefits before they commit or how you structure your guarantee can differentiate you and create buyer preference.

The how can also be used to help you to create a personalized experience for your customers. That way they are treated as unique individuals and not as a member of a mass market.

CHAPTER 7 THE FOURTH BIG QUESTION OF BUSINESS SUCCESS IS WHERE?

Again, this can be an easy way to create a differentiated offer since it can be where your customers are or where you are based. Before the Internet, many businesses were able to differentiate themselves because they were the only people in their area who offered the particular product or service. Many still can if location or transportation are important issues.

It's been said for many years that the three golden rules of retailing are location, location and location.

There are two types of stores:

Destination stores - which customers will go out of their way to reach, and
Passing stores - business comes from people walking past and being enticed in.

It may seem strange but sometimes being located next to a competitor is a big plus factor for the customer.

Look at the real estate agents and car dealerships in your area and you'll find that they often cluster together, creating a stronger magnet to potential customers than any one supplier can do on its own.

Sometimes location is a big sign of quality. In London, top medical professionals gather together in Harley Street and prestige tailors are in Saville Row in Mayfair.

Specialization (what) and choice of customers (who) is then needed to create differentiation among those in the same location.

Where the product comes from or has been made can also be used as a differentiation factor. One of the vodka companies had success emphasizing that it was genuine because it was made in Russia and not at a local plant to a standard recipe.

Where is also factor in one of the most remarkable marketing achievements -branding bottled water and persuading people to pay a premium price when there is a close substitute you can get for free out of the tap?

Where can also be used to describe where your products are made available. L'eggs pantyhose and tights broke away from the traditional distribution channels and went into supermarkets.

Other products maintain exclusivity by only making products available through approved dealers who have the image or service to support their promotion. These products are deliberately kept out of the supermarkets. Tesco lost a court case against Levi Strauss for selling trademarked products without permission.

Where can also be used to create differentiation by where you advertise and promote your business. Many products - even in the Internet age - generate sales because they are seen as unique by customers who don't know better, even if they are imitators themselves or have been imitated.

It's what your customer perceives that matters and if your customer thinks your product is unique, because it's the only one they are aware of, and they buy, then you've created differentiation through your choice of marketing channel. This is why outreach marketing can still work if customers don't then search for a generic solution, once their interest has been raised.

Finally, your product or service can be differentiated on the where dimension by changing where it is delivered.

Instead of going to buy vegetables at the shops, imagine having a seasonal local vegetable box delivered every week.
The fifth big question of business success is when.

As well as being in the Internet age, we are also in the "I want it now" age. Speed matters.
When can you deliver - and is the time guaranteed?

When can you start the service? Or even more important, when do you think you will have finished?

FedEx is a giant business built on the concept of reliable speed and their tagline "When it absolutely, positively has to be there overnight" is a textbook example of a great USP or marketing slogan.

One of the reasons why I love Amazon is the consistent quick deliveries and they let me choose how important speed is to me with their delivery options.

Unreliable promises are a major problem. Who hasn't taken time off work for a home service or delivery, only to find that it never came? Speed and reliability go hand in hand.

If you're selling business to business, your aim is to help your customer to make more money by selling more, at higher prices or by reducing costs.

Stock or inventory in the distribution system is expensive and just in time techniques can create major cost savings. The slower the lead time between ordering and delivery and the more unreliable the time period, the more stock the customer has to carry. If the customer under-stocks and experiences stock-outs, they lose sales opportunities.

For a product which offers a clear financial return, an important when question is when is the financial payback? By that I mean when does the customer get their money back and move into funds? Until then, buying has made them worse off and they know it.

When can also be used to focus on when you introduce products into the market. There are major advantages in being the first mover and creating a reputation for innovative solutions.

There are also costs involved and some businesses prefer to be rapid second movers with a product that is better, more reliable or has extra features and benefits.

CHAPTER 7 THE SIXTH BIG QUESTION OF BUSINESS SUCCESS IS WHY?

The entire subject of differentiating your business is designed to answer the key why question... Why should I buy from you rather than one of your competitors?

I use the why question to focus attention on why you're in business doing what you do?
People emotionally connect to businesses with a story and a clear purpose. A business with a personal cause creates a strong impression.

I remember meeting a young entrepreneur who had started a nursing home for elderly people. It began because he was looking for a place to look after his grandmother and he was shocked by what he saw.

Rather than just having a moan, he saw the problem, the pain that poor care caused and decided to do something about it. He created a nursing home with standards of care good enough for his own grandma.

And doesn't that purpose sound more appealing than "I started the nursing home because I saw it as an easy way to make a lot of money."

My own obsession with what makes a small business successful goes back to my early days as a trainee accountant in the early eighties recession.

I got to see behind the mask of "business is great" that you hear so often when you're networking. I saw plenty of nice people struggling to earn a good living, even though they were committed to giving their customers a good deal.

I am fascinated by why this happens and want to make the critical difference.

I also saw businesses that were very successful, also owned and managed by nice people so I knew big profits didn't depend on the ruthless "out for whatever you can get" approach you see in TV shows like the Apprentice and films like Wall Street.

Sometimes a business ties directly into a major cause.

I had a client who sells machines which condense high quality water from the atmosphere - it has a strong environmental appeal in developed countries and an even more fundamental "right to clean water" offer in the poorest places in the world.

Or a business can be focused on relieving significant pain and distress for customers, like the nursing home I mentioned.

Other times you can borrow a cause by linking your business to a major charity. I've done it with a cancer charity because I wanted to give back and say thank you.

The why can be even smaller. I know people who only buy charity Christmas cards. The donation may be small but it's the thought that counts. If it creates customer preference, then it's differentiation.

CHAPTER 8 THE SEVENTH BIG QUESTION OF BUSINESS SUCCESS IS HOW MANY?

When you're differentiating your business, you are moving away from competing on price.

Customers buy based on perceived value for money. In answering how many questions you shift the focus away from the monetary sacrifice to the value the customers get in return for their money.

One simple way is to give more of what the customer is buying.

You see this in the mobile telephone market.

The minimum monthly tariff may be the same across different competitors but what you get for your money in terms of calls, texts and internet access is different.

Particular packages appeal to different types of users. I make telephone calls, but I don't text so the number of text messages in the offer is irrelevant to me. Others are astonished that I speak to people when they send a flurry of text messages. You also see it in catering in the "eat as much as you want" lunchtime offer or the bottomless cup of coffee.

When you're thinking about differentiating on the how many dimensions, you can easily move to how big.

Size doesn't matter for just food. Sony went the other way and have developed outstanding capabilities for miniaturization. A big part of the appeal of my iPod is that I am able to carry around my big collection of classic rock CDs.

There we have it.

The seven big questions of business success but I want to share a few thoughts about the big question eight we've been avoiding; how much is your price?

Having a low price can create a strong purchase preference for standard goods but only if the customers believe the goods really are of comparable quality.

Often the customer can't judge quality or value until after purchase and consumption. In these situations, price can become a short cut guide to quality.

And a low price implies low quality.

I can't tell you how many times I've gone into a supermarket and rejected things because they are too cheap. I compare the price of one item to another and if the difference is small, I may buy on price.

But if the difference is big, it acts as a big red flag against the cheapest item. There has to be some reason why it's so cheap.

Some customers are price constrained. They don't have the money to buy at high prices.

Others are value constrained and know that if the item isn't fit for purpose, they've wasted their money.

Some customers even get pleasure from buying the most expensive which creates an interesting way to differentiate yourself.

Instead of thinking about how much in terms of how to be the cheapest, you could think about how much the other way around.

Do you want an interesting experience for lunch and a story to tell people about?

What about trying the world's most expensive cheese sandwich. Created in 2010 by Michelin starred chef Martin Blunos it cost £110.59. Its main ingredients are cheddar blended with white truffles and sprinkled with edible gold dust.

To summarize, you need to differentiate your business to create customer preference which isn't based on lowest prices.

You do it by uniquely meeting the wants and needs of your customers.

I've gone through the seven big questions of business success - what, who, how, where, when, why and how many and shared a few ideas and examples.

Use these questions as a framework to design your business.

You'll find that there are other angles that I haven't covered because I want to keep the recording short.

CHAPTER 9 THERE ARE A FEW POINTS I WANT TO EMPHASIZE.

The first is that you need to be differentiated in ways that customers value. You can be different in ways that don't matter. That can be a distraction for you, your customers and a waste of time, energy and money. If you're looking for advice on how to differentiate your business, you don't care whether I'm 7 foot eight tall or 3 foot 4. I can be the biggest or the smallest business coach but it's irrelevant because you want my ideas and methods.

Second, you don't need one big difference. The difference between winning a gold or silver medal at the Olympics may be a fraction of a second. The difference between being first or second choice for a buyer may be equally tight - what matters is that you are first choice for a good proportion and not second choice for all.

The concept of the USP or unique selling proposition can be daunting to business owners. Even in the global, Internet connected world we live in, you don't need to be unique in the world. Your customer doesn't have perfect knowledge of every possible option and doesn't have the time or inclination to do a lot of research. Your task is to appear unique in the five or ten options he or she considers. Remember if your customers perceives your business as unique, then they will act as if you are.

Take the time to think about some of your strongest buying preferences and you'll see that in some cases it can be one thing that wins, in others it is being slightly better in a number of important attributes.

Third, the way your differences fit together must be consistent so that they reinforce each other. You don't want to attract one group of customers with one element of your offer and repel them with another. It helps to focus your business around a few different customer situations and personas rather than adding elements into the mix to appeal to a wide variety of people.

Fourth, don't ignore costs. Some of the ways you can differentiate your business are free - for example deciding to focus your business on a particular type of customer -but differentiation often costs money. Your aim is to differentiate in ways that increase your profit and that means that customers must be willing to pay a price premium. That doesn't mean you have to charge a higher price. You can reap the rewards of extra volume by offering better value for the same price. Costs on everything you do that doesn't influence your differentiation factors need to be kept low.

Fifth, to create a long-term advantage, your differentiation must be hard to copy or you must be willing to keep taking the next step before your competitors. Since differentiation has to be perceived by customers for it to be of any value, it is also visible to competitors. But how you do it can be a mystery. Some forms of differentiation are very easy to copy and if it leads to success, some of your competitors will be tempted to copy unless the move creates extra costs or inconsistencies internally or externally.

Let's imagine you have two main competitors.

Firm A also wants to be differentiated and will deliberately choose to target different types of customers or provide different solutions. You respect each other's space because you both know that you can gain preference with enough buyers.

Firm B wants to straddle your position and Firm A. It may be able to add the features and benefits that appeal to both sets of customers and therefore appeal to a bigger, wider market. But B can only do so by increasing its costs so if it wants to match your prices, it must accept a lower margin.

Alternatively, the very act of trying to straddle may create conflicts and complications.

Imagine you are a world class athlete and you are very talented at many events -sprinting, jumping, throwing and middle-distance running.

You can compete as a generalist in the decathlon and win, or you can specialize in one event. What you can't do is compete as a generalist and a specialist because the muscle building exercises to improve your throwing add on extra weight which harms your ability in the high jump and running the 1500 meters.

It's the same in business and I often see the mistake of claiming too many specialties. This is very common in the building industry and professional services. The customers don't believe any small business can be great at everything, leading to the inevitable "jack of all trades, master of none" conclusion.

CHAPTER 10 MEET THE PERFECT CUSTOMER LIFECYCLE

The Perfect Customer Lifecycle provides guidance to small businesses searching for a simpler way to develop a marketing plan. No expensive books and workshops. No complicated forms and exercises. No gimmicky sales jargon. Just seven simple steps that act as a framework for developing your sales and marketing process.

Attract Traffic | Capture Leads | Nurture Prospects | Convert Sales | Deliver & Satisfy | Upsell Customers | Get Referrals

Using the Perfect Customer Lifecycle, you can create a marketing plan designed to measurably grow your business through targeted communication and smarter lead management, leading to better lead conversion rates, increased sales and greater profits.

Now that you understand the importance of developing a clear, structured marketing plan, let's dig a little deeper into each of the steps.

STEP 1: ATTRACT TRAFFIC

Consumers today have become highly adept at ignoring advertising in all its forms—they skip TV commercials, stream free online radio, block emails from unknown senders and are virtually blind to banner ads. Paid advertising alone is no longer a viable option for driving traffic to your website; you have to earn traffic by creating valuable content that attracts visitors.

Content can mean many things to many people, but really it's any valuable piece of information or entertainment that attracts leads to your site.

Some content is naturally prone to lead generation purposes, such as reports and webinars. For example, if you sell interior design software, you could write a report called "10 Tricks for Better Space Planning." Other content could focus more on brand awareness, such as a blog post titled "2012 Forecast on Colors in Interior Design."

In both cases, you'll attract traffic to your website with the lure of valuable information. More importantly, you'll start to develop a trusted relationship with your visitors. When creating a content library, it's best to create one piece at a time. Before you know it, you'll have built a body of work that raises your brand equity and serves to generate leads and raving fans.

Once you have content in place, you want people to find it. Here are a few ideas to get you started.

Get Discovered with SEO

SEO (search engine optimization) is the process of getting your content and website found when people perform searches on sites such as Google or Yahoo. Better search engine rankings mean you get seen by more people—and that increases traffic to your website.

Get Results with PPC

Paid advertising, or Pay-Per-Click (PPC), enables you to boost online traffic by paying a fixed amount to promote link clicks to your content and website. The best ways to get started in paid advertising are through Google AdWords and Facebook Ads.

Google AdWords

Google is the simplest and most well-known platform for PPC advertising. Basically, you bid on keywords that are most relevant to your business, and then pay Google a certain amount for each time someone clicks on your ad. The more popular the keyword, the higher the per-click price.

Facebook Ads

Facebook is second only to Google in terms of site visitors per day. Where Google allows you to target based on what people are searching for, Facebook allows you to select what type of people your ad will be served to—say, yoga enthusiasts or moms in a certain ZIP code. Recently Facebook has outperformed AdWords in results.

Get Social

Social media doesn't have to be daunting. And since 75% of consumers use social media in some format to learn about products and services, you can't afford to not be in the social sphere. Start a blog to talk about new products, industry news or company updates. Reward Twitter followers or customers who "Like" you on Facebook with exclusive offers and specials. And maintain your B2B connections on LinkedIn. All of these services are free and easy to manage with only a little effort. The keys to successful social engagement are being consistent and being real.

STEP 2 CAPTURE LEADS

Now that you're attracting people to your website with the lure of valuable content, you need to entice them to give you their contact information so you can nurture them over time. Web forms are an excellent way to capture leads, but the reality for most small businesses is that the majority of their website visitors never submit a form. If this is the case for your site, there could be several factors dissuading people from opting in.

Your Content Isn't Compelling

For visitors to fill out a Web form, they must be motivated enough to share their personal information and take the time to consume the content. If your opt-in rates are low, it could be because your content doesn't seem to offer enough value.

The best content is informative and original. Content that is fluffy or simply rehashed from somewhere else will not perform well. Many businesses have a newsletter sign-up form, but this is becoming less effective as people look for ways to reduce the number of emails they receive in an already overloaded inbox. If you do offer a newsletter, be clear about the benefits of subscribing.

Make sure the way you describe your content motivates visitors to act. To do this, use a strong headline that entices them to action, clearly state the benefits of the content and help them feel rewarded for taking action.

You Ask for Too Much Information

Consumers are becoming more protective of their time and personal information. To maximize opt-ins, minimize the number of required fields on your forms. Typically, name and email are sufficient. If you sell to other businesses, you may also want to capture company name. A good rule of thumb is that the more information you ask for, the more value you need to provide. You can always ask for more data as your relationship grows.

You Don't Inspire Trust

If a visitor is reluctant to submit a form on your website, it could be because your site doesn't look credible enough. When a prospect visits your website, they should sense that you offer a comfortable level of expertise. Anything less means that they will continue to shop around until they find someone who inspires confidence. Demonstrating expertise can be as simple as including customer testimonials or case studies, mentioning industry awards, listing credentials and certifications and linking to your privacy policy.

STEP 3: NURTURE PROSPECTS

The truth is, most buyers don't see an ad and immediately purchase your product. They buy when they are ready to buy. To reach these buyers, you need a systematic approach for developing trust and converting leads. The not-so-secret weakness of small businesses is that they don't follow up with leads as well as they should. But consistent, valuable follow-up messages can prove to be a huge competitive edge, as long as you approach the nurturing process with a clear communications plan in mind.

Set Frequency Expectations

Customers who opt into your communications want to hear from you, but they don't want to be overwhelmed by hyper-frequent communications. Create a consistent timeline for your campaign that fulfills the needs and wishes of your customers as well as your business. It's best to set your customers' expectations upfront—for example, "Sign up for our monthly newsletter" or "Get our weekly specials." If you have an online storefront, for example, you may want to send weekly emails with new products or a limited-time sale. If you're a motivational speaker, a monthly newsletter might be a better approach. Daily emails are almost never a good idea unless your subscriber is expecting it.

Personalize Your Communications

Studies show that customers respond better to communications that are personalized to them. Evaluate your follow-up communications—whether email, direct mail or other methods—and

Chris Gold

determine how you can customize them to each person in your database. It could be as simple as using their first name or as targeted as suggesting products based on past purchases.

STEP 4: CONVERT SALES

You can attract, capture and nurture all the leads you'd like, but if they don't convert into paying customers, you're not going to make any money. Depending on your business type and setup, you likely use one of two methods for converting leads into customers: an online shopping cart or a sales team. No matter which method you use, there are a few strategies to realize the full potential of both.

E-Commerce Shopping Carts

Your online shopping cart represents your digital storefront and should be as effective and easy to use as someone visiting a brick-and-mortar store. However, there are some advantages of selling online that can't be realized in a typical retail environment.

First, an online shopping cart gives you the ability to intelligently upsell customers to increase transaction amounts. Upsell offers are most effective when they are closely related to the current order. A good cart will present an upsell offer in a clean, sensible fashion that allows customers to easily add additional products to their purchase. Some shopping cart systems will even allow you to offer multiple upsell offers.

The second advantage of selling online is that you can use targeted campaigns to invite people back to your store if they leave before making a purchase. The most effective campaigns generally offer a discount on the products the customer was viewing.

Personal Selling

For some companies, customers must connect with a salesperson before making a purchase. Unfortunately, many of these sales-intensive businesses lose revenue because of a buy-or-die mentality on the sales floor. If a lead comes in that isn't ready to engage right away, it can fall into a black hole of lost leads that could have become customers given enough time and nurturing. These wasted opportunities add up to a lot of lost revenue in the long run.

To prevent this, you must be able to nurture leads and identify when they are ready to distribute to your salesperson. Your sales team is a valuable resource, the driving force behind growing your business. They can be much more effective if your CRM automatically evaluates certain behaviors and factors, identifies hot leads and intelligently distributes them based on specific factors such as industry and geography.

In addition, every day your sales team engages in dozens of communications with leads. Automating some of these communications could free up your team to focus on only high-impact conversations instead of routine follow-up messages. This type of workflow automation can be used to automatically add notes to records, send thank you notes after sales calls and kick off educational emails and more. The best part is, by leveraging workflow automation to save time, your sales team starts to view your CRM system as a valuable resource—and not just a waste of time.

It takes an average of five sales calls to close a deal, but most salespeople give up after just one or two calls

STEP 5: DELIVER AND SATISFY

If you have ever received disappointing customer service (and who hasn't?), you won't be surprised to learn that most companies spend more on acquiring new customers than keeping existing ones happy.

Winning lifelong customers requires the ability to not only get a prospect to buy again and again, but to do so happily. The benefits go far beyond inspiring loyalty and repeat business; happy customers become advocates for your brand, driving referrals by sharing their experiences with friends, colleagues and social networks.

Service as a Marketing Strategy

Great customer service is a HUGE competitive advantage. Say you need something fixed at your office. Company A was an hour late, talked on their cell phone the whole time and left without telling you they were done. Company B, on the other hand, arrived on time, explained what they were going to do to fix your problem and gave you a coupon for your next service. Which company will you use next time?

The same warm, friendly, accommodating approach you take to nurture a customer should be continued for the duration of the relationship. Positive experiences lead to repeat business and referrals. Service as a strategy has to come from the top and be truly ingrained in your company's core values. Every process, every decision, every employee must act in alignment with this strategy in order to be successful.

Deliver as Promised—Automatically

Despite their best intentions, many small businesses over-promise and under-deliver simply because they don't have enough time and energy to meet the expectations set during the sales and marketing process. Luckily, many elements of great customer service can be automated, which eases the burden on the business and helps customers feel valued and appreciated.

For example, a big customer service challenge for many businesses is training customers on how to successfully use their product. Instead of training customers in person or over the phone, which requires a big commitment from both parties, automation allows you to create engagement campaigns that slowly drip information over time.

Another advantage of automation is that it allows you to easily identify and segment happy and unhappy customers through a simple survey. Customers who are satisfied can be automatically rerouted to a testimonial and referral campaign while unsatisfied customers can be routed to customer service for personal follow-up.

STEP 6: UPSELL CUSTOMERS

One of the very first statistics business owners learn is this: 80% of your profits come from the top 20% of your customers. Yet so many small business owners spend all their time focusing on attracting and converting new leads and customers that upsell and cross-sell efforts directed at existing customers completely fall off the radar.

As we've shared in the previous steps of the Perfect Customer Lifecycle, consistent communication with customers is essential—and this shouldn't end once a first sale is made.

Customers who had a positive experience with your company are more likely to think of you the next time they need a similar product or service. Continue to develop relationships through lead nurturing, like letting customers know about complementary products and services they might enjoy.

The best way to accomplish this is to create automated follow-up campaigns based on a scheduled sequence that continues to communicate with customers in the form of emails or direct mail and other offline methods. You could even target these communications to feature new products, services or promotions based on your customers' previous buying history, ensuring you're always delivering something of value.

STEP 7: GET REFERRALS

Once you've established a clear process for funneling leads from their first contact to after-purchase communications, you're in a great position for the final step in the Perfect Customer Lifecycle: growing even more through customer referrals and affiliates.

Get Customer Referrals

People are more likely to do business with someone when they're introduced by a mutual acquaintance. Based on that idea, customer referral programs are a fantastic way to generate highly qualified leads. The key to getting referrals from happy customers is simple—just ask. And don't forget to reward customers for their referrals with a thank you gift, account credit or heartfelt thank you card.

Leverage Affiliates

Affiliates are third parties who market your product on their website and through email and social media. They are an excellent way to drive traffic to your website and generate leads. The best thing about affiliate programs is the ROI—you pay only for performance. You simply make a small investment in marketing resources and then pay affiliates for any leads or sales they generate. Because your investment is minimal, these programs can yield amazing returns.

Motivate Partners to Act

When developing referral and affiliate programs, it's important to clearly outline what you hope to achieve and provide the right incentives to encourage participation. A partner's reason for participating is not always all about money. Take time to understand those motivations and develop incentives that best suit those needs—and your own. Think back to Step 5: Deliver and Satisfy. The same principles we outlined for making customers happy should be applied to your partners—always deliver as promised. So, Are You Ready for Business Coaching?

As an owner, you have to ask yourself if you're coachable — or at least willing to be coached.

That means admitting you don't know everything. It also means being willing to implement new and sometimes uncomfortable ideas for you and your company.

You also need to be willing to do the work necessary to grow the company. Why? Because unlike a consultant who may do a project and leave, your Business Coach will educate you on strategy and process — and leave it to you to implement.

Your coach won't do the work but will expect the work to get done. For the coaching process, that's where accountability comes in and is key to your achievement and your company's ultimate success.

Good Luck!

www.ingramcontent.com/pod-product-compliance
Lightning Source LLC
Chambersburg PA
CBHW070901220526
45466CB00005B/2074